POSTCARD HISTORY SERIES

Onset and
Point Independence

ONSET & PT. INDEPENDENCE
Cape Cod

Onset and Point Independence occupy the northerly shores of Onset Bay, an arm of Buzzards Bay in southeastern Massachusetts. In the center of this image, the Point Independence Bridge connects its namesake village on the right bank of the East River with Onset where the pier that interrupts the arc of white sand marking Onset Beach is visible. Opposite Point Independence is Wicket's Island. Onset Island (right) marks the entrance to Buzzards Bay. (Author's collection.)

ON THE FRONT COVER: One of the most scenic views at Onset is the vista over Onset Bay from Bay View Grove. Here, atop the bluffs beneath towering oaks and pines, visitors historically took in a panorama that included Point Independence, Onset Island, Wicket's Island, Lydia's Island, and Shell Point, as well as activity on Steamboat Wharf and Onset Beach below. Today, this same view continues to enchant. (Courtesy of Kenneth R. Maddigan.)

ON THE BACK COVER: Long a landmark in Onset Bay, wooded Wicket's Island with its 40-foot sandy bluffs is not only a scenic focal point, but also is ecologically and culturally significant, having associations with the area's earliest inhabitants and Onset's 19th-century development as a Spiritualist community. In October 2015, the Town of Wareham and the Buzzards Bay Coalition moved to permanently preserve the island. (Author's collection.)

POSTCARD HISTORY SERIES

Onset and Point Independence

Michael J. Maddigan

ARCADIA
PUBLISHING

Published by Arcadia Publishing
Charleston, South Carolina

Printed in the United States of America

Library of Congress Control Number: 2015959125

For all general information contact Arcadia Publishing at:
Telephone 843-853-2070
Fax 843-853-0044
E-mail sales@arcadiapublishing.com
For customer service and orders:
Toll-Free 1-888-313-2665

Visit us on the Internet at www.arcadiapublishing.com

CONTENTS

ACKNOWLEDGMENTS

The author wishes to thank the staff of the Wareham Free Library for their assistance in locating resources relating to Onset and their helpfulness on this project. Thanks also go to Erin Vosgien and the team at Arcadia Publishing for shepherding this book from a proposal through to a final product. Special thanks go to Kenneth R. Maddigan, who loaned several postcards from the collection he started in 1978 with his father, the late Albert T. Maddigan. Ken, like his dad, has a great affection for Point Independence and Onset, and I wish to thank him for his generosity, enthusiasm, and kindliness. Unless otherwise noted, all images appear courtesy of the author.

INTRODUCTION

Established in 1877 as a summer camp meeting ground by a group of eastern Massachusetts Spiritualists who believed in communication with the dead, Onset Bay Grove soon emerged as the leading Spiritualist summer community in the nation and was often described as the "Spiritualists' Summer Home by the Sea." Campgoers attended lectures, conferences, and séances in search of enlightenment. Under the influence of Spiritualism, Onset quickly developed from a collection of tents to a village of small, wood-frame cottages that provided a greater degree of comfort for those coming to the grove. For those without cottages of their own, hotels and rooming houses provided accommodation while restaurants furnished board as well as refreshment for the ever-increasing number of sightseers attracted by the scenery, cool breezes, or simple curiosity.

Unlike their counterparts elsewhere who attended camp meetings conducted by the orthodox religions that deemed the sacred nature of these meetings incompatible with recreational activities, Onset Spiritualists unabashedly enjoyed the opportunities the area afforded, including bathing in warm ocean waters, sailing, fishing, attending concerts and theatrical productions, bowling, roller skating, and cycling. Though a series of embarrassing scandals in the late 1800s damaged the reputation of Onset Spiritualism, it was the influx of summer visitors seeking recreational opportunities rather than religious revelation that led to the decline of Spiritualism's influence locally and Onset's subsequent development as a secular resort community after 1900.

Having shed its Spiritualist origins, Onset continued to expand, streetcar railways fostering its growth. In 1913, the Onset Board of Trade began actively promoting Onset as a resort and commercial center through publication of tourist brochures and promotional literature while the post–World War I arrival of the automobile brought day-trippers in droves to see what the advertising was all about. What they found was a dynamic community where summers were devoted to life on, in, and about the sea. Catering to the needs and wants of the community was the small but vibrant Onset Avenue commercial district, where traditional stores stood alongside souvenir stands and the village's three moving picture houses.

Spurred by the rapacious growth of Onset, Point Independence developed in the late 1880s and early 1890s across the East River as a resort devoid of any hint of Spiritualism. Though sometimes referred to as a "suburb" of Onset, Point Independence had an identity of its own and eventually a separate post office to prove it.

In contrast to high-toned resorts elsewhere, Onset and Point Independence remained strictly middle class. As early as 1882 the New Bedford *Standard* remarked upon this, reporting that "one of the chief charms of this beautiful place is the spirit of hospitality and open-heartedness everywhere prevalent. The people do not seem to possess any of the exclusiveness found in too many watering-places." The *Boston Globe* later called Onset the "summer home of the common people," the "people's resort," and "the Coney Island of the South Shore," noting a proud lack of pretension that survives to this day.

Onset and Point Independence's heyday as a secular tourist center between 1900 and 1940 coincided with the golden age of postcards. Picture postcards marketed to a largely transitory audience captured the development of Onset and Point Independence during this era while reinforcing the villages' resort credentials. Picture postcards, however, did not depict the reality of life at Onset but rather life as vacationists wished to recall it—scenic and escapist. Left undocumented were stories of people and events that helped shape Onset and Point Independence, including the Cape Verdean community that first came to the area in the 1890s. As a result, the focus of this history—Onset and Point Independence's development as a resort community in the first half of the 20th century—is necessarily dictated by the nature of images on the mass-produced cards. And though this is but one of many stories that can be told of Onset and Point Independence, it is both an important and a fascinating one.

A series of unfortunate events contributed to the post–World War II decline of Onset, including the Great Depression, devastating hurricanes between 1938 and 1954, the construction of the Bourne Bridge and the rerouting of traffic away from Onset, a 1946 murder and explosion in the center of the village, the discontinuation of train service to Wareham, and new vacation habits of postwar America. Matters were not helped by the sometimes difficult relationship with Wareham, which culminated in unsuccessful efforts to secede in 1949.

While Onset had been previously untroubled by its identity as a summer resort, construction and promotion of competing modern resort amenities along Route 28 on Cape Cod beginning in the late 1940s prompted some to question Onset's sense of self and the validity of its claim to be a "Cape resort." Was Onset part of Cape Cod or not? The Provincetown *Advocate* addressed this issue and seemed to favor Onset's inclusion. "A reader took us to task the other day for saying in a news story that Onset was on the Cape. And yet Onset is a village in Wareham, and Wareham certainly has as many scrub pines and cranberry bogs and nearly as much frontage on Buzzards Bay as Bourne or Falmouth." The Yarmouth *Register* disagreed. "Maybe we can't blame such towns as Wareham or Onset for trying to be part of Cape Cod, after all, they are pretty close, but they still aren't the real thing. It is futile for them to try, if not downright ridiculous." Most argued that the Cape began at the Cape Cod Canal, thereby excluding Onset. And while the matter might seem irrelevant, Onset's exclusion from the Cape meant that it failed to share the prestige of the Cape resorts, and mid-20th-century tourists began to dismiss it as hopelessly old-fashioned. Bypassed by tourists in their haste to get to the "true" Cape, Onset was forgotten.

Fortunately, this trend has been arrested, and Onset is experiencing a renaissance and a rediscovery. No longer promoting itself strictly as the easily accessible alternative to Cape Cod, emphasis is now placed upon the characteristics and activities that make Onset and Point Independence distinctive: the large number of family-oriented events during the summer season, the villages' rich Victorian architectural heritage, and always the beaches and the bay.

Today, visitors continue to be drawn to Onset and Point Independence for the same reasons described by author and columnist Frank P. Sibley over a century ago. Writing in 1909, Sibley noted the quiet allure of Onset, which still continues to ensnare unwary visitors:

> The charm of Onset is rather subtle. There is, of course, the usual routine of amusements, such as may be found at every summer place—the motors, the power boats, the sailing and fishing, the open-air theatres, to which the "trippers" . . . go with gusto.
>
> But there is beyond all this a softness, a wholesomeness in the air, a homely sort of attractiveness in the gentle hills and foreshortened shrubbery, a clean sense of well-being on the clean sands, that all draw the person who is attracted not at all by the noisier and more popular forms of amusements.
>
> Onset, once it has gripped a person by its charm, does not easily let him go again.

One

Onset Bluffs and Bay View Grove

Along the Bluffs, Onset, Mass.

Onset was noted for its tree-covered bluffs that rose above the bay, extending from Shell Point to the East River. A principal attraction that drew the Spiritualists to Onset, the bluffs were reserved as public lands in the 1870s by the Onset Bay Grove Association, which developed the location. Writers of the period spoke of glimpses of the glittering bay caught from beneath the shady canopy of pines and oaks.

The sandy bluffs were one of the principal attractions of early Onset, and narrow footpaths meandered along their crest between spots where views could be had over Onset Bay and the beach below. Plank sidewalks along the boulevards adjoining the bluffs made easier walking for some. The promenade extended for a mile and a half above the bay. (Courtesy of Kenneth R. Maddigan.)

PATH ALONG THE BLUFFS, ONSET, MASS.

In 1879, Edward S. Wheeler of Philadelphia wrote in the Spiritualist journal *Mind and Matter* describing Onset. "There, for a rarity, forest and shore are co-joined, and the bold, semicircular bluffs catch the sea breezes from every direction . . . A walk over the planks may be had for the moiety of a mile, and by day or night, in sun or moonlight, the view is 'a thing of beauty and a joy forever.' "

BAND CONCERT TIME, ONSET BAY, MASS.

An 1881 correspondent for the *Barnstable Patriot* was equally rhapsodic in his praise for Onset and its groves that invited picnickers and concertgoers: "There is no more attractive place on the Southern shore of this State than Onset Bay and its vicinity. . . There are singular natural beauties and advantages on the eastern Wareham shores which those who have not been there would be surprised to see."

In Bay View Grove, Onset, Mass.

"At Onset Bay one will be agreeably disappointed at the perfection of the situation," continued the *Barnstable Patriot* writer enthusiastically. "The points, and bluffs, and knobs; the bays and coves and indentations; the sheltering woodlands and inviting shores, make up a fullness and completeness of things enjoyable and enticing." Many came simply to experience the views from Bay View Grove (pictured), Onset Avenue, and South Boulevard.

The various small parks that dotted the grounds were equipped with numerous benches and seats, which invited sitting, and clusters of people throughout the grounds could be frequently seen enjoying the scenery and sights or engaging in thoughtful discussion. Bay View Grove at Onset Avenue and South Boulevard was the first area of the parklike bluff to be developed in Onset, being cleared of undergrowth in 1877.

A correspondent for the *Boston Globe* in 1882 praised Bay View Grove's natural setting: "Nature, to be sure, is doing her share to make the place more attractive. No summer resort along the eastern coast of Massachusetts can begin to boast of the natural advantages that exist in comparison with Onset Bay. The historical old oaks and pines standing out, as it were, in bold relief."

Watching the Bathers, Onset, Mass.

Solid middle-class families were drawn to the recreational opportunities Onset afforded, many of which could be had for free. Walking along the bluff, bathing in the sea, and enjoying a picnic lunch were all entertainments that cost nothing. Many, like the visitors here in Bay View Grove overlooking the main beach, came to listen to a concert or merely to watch the crowds.

WATCHING THE BATHERS,
ONSET, MASS.

Onset's parks and scenic vistas became threatened when the Onset Bay Grove Association began leasing the open grounds for development in the 1890s. Opposing this was the Onset Protective League, founded in 1897, which asserted the public's right of access. Following a lengthy court case (1899–1915), the Supreme Judicial Court of Massachusetts decreed in 1916 that the bluffs, including Bay View Grove, were to remain forever open to public use.

ON THE BLUFFS, ONSET BAY, MASS.

Protected permanently from development, Bay View Grove and the surrounding bluffs continued to attract excursionists. Initially, improvements to the grounds were funded by a $2 surchage on property owners; following 1916, the open spaces were maintained as public parks by the Town of Wareham. Under the direction of the Park Commission, plantings, including beautiful flower beds, and other enhancements were made annually.

A SUNDAY AFTERNOON AT ONSET, MASS.

The bandstand was an early addition to Bay View Grove, and it became the venue for regular concerts featuring bands from throughout the region. As indicated by this view looking across Onset Avenue, concerts on Sundays, the one day most visitors had free from work, were popular. Destroyed during the 1944 hurricane, the bandstand was not rebuilt until a few years after the war. (Courtesy of Kenneth R. Maddigan.)

Automobiles like those seen here at the base of Bay View Grove brought new visitors who came to enjoy the view of Onset Bay, its sparkling waters, and the white sails of boats. In the background (right) is Steamboat Wharf with Kenny's Salt Water Taffy stand. When the postcard was mailed in 1917, Kenny's was the sole building permitted to remain on the beach. (Courtesy of Kenneth R. Maddigan.)

The myriad of activities available to post–World War I Onset visitors included sailing, boating, bathing, concerts, strolling, and automobiling. Bay View Grove, with its commanding position above the Steamboat Wharf and recently built Town Pier, both seen here about 1919, remained a central gathering point and a popular locale for the observation of boat races on the bay.

A View of the Park,   Onset, Cape Cod, Mass.

When Bay View Grove, Shell Point Grove, and the Onset bluffs were developed, stands of oaks and pines were left intact. Today, the trees are more sparse thanks to several hurricanes between 1938 and 1954. Though the Wareham Park Department replanted fallen trees in Bay View Grove, these did not grow easily, as indicated by a 1948 town report lamenting the difficulty of growing replacements on the bluff.

Onset Bay, Mass., The Bluffs.

Onset Avenue east of Union Avenue runs along the crest of the bluffs and has long been a whirl of activity. The principal sites of the Spiritualist camp meeting grounds, including the Onset Bay Grove Association's Headquarters Building and the open-air auditorium (now the Lillian Gregerman Band Shell), were located here, as well as Onset's earliest and largest hotels and Steamboat Wharf (now Onset Pier).

ASSOCIATION BUILDING, ONSET BAY.   Issued by Holmes' Casino, Onset, Mass.

Built in 1884 opposite Bay View Grove, the Headquarters Building of the Onset Bay Grove Association still stands on Onset Avenue. An early visitor remarked, "The pagoda-like upper story adds to its architectural beauty, and it has been very properly utilized as a sleeping room" by the Association's president H.B. Storer. The second story room was fitted for séances. The first floor housed offices where Spiritualist literature was sold.

Greetings from Onset Beach, Massachusetts
U. S. O.

The Headquarters Building was originally painted red, white, and blue, one newspaper reporting "it is quite gaudily painted . . . but that seems to be in order at all new seashore or summer places." During World War II, the building served as a USO facility. It subsequently housed Howard Johnson's, Harbor Lights restaurant, and Dunkin' Donuts, and is now home to the Quahog Republic and Guido's Ice Cream.

HOLMES' CASINO, ONSET.   Issued by Holmes' Casino, Onset, Mass.

Initially used as a restaurant, the casino, built in 1893 on Onset Avenue east of the Headquarters Building, was owned by George C. Holmes of Brockton. Holmes sold and rented bathing suits, fishing tackle, soda, cigars, and newspapers, and held the public bathing privilege in 1895, with 20 bathhouses on the beach below. Also housed in the building were billiard rooms.

ONSET AVENUE, ONSET, MASS.

Holmes promoted Onset through publication of souvenir booklets and postcards (several of which appear in this volume). As an agent for Eastman Kodak, he also photographed, developed, and printed images. "A photograph of your cottage, or a group of friends and relatives, makes a lasting souvenir of a pleasant season," he advertised. The casino was destroyed on July 21, 1921, by a fire set to cover a robbery. (Courtesy of Kenneth R. Maddigan.)

The bluffs continued eastward from Bay View Grove and Steamboat Wharf to the East River, also known historically as Swift's River. The bluffs here were especially popular, given the presence of two large resort hotels, the Onset Hotel and the Glen Cove House. Views could be had over Onset Bay towards Buzzards Bay, seen between Onset and Wicket's Islands. (Courtesy of Kenneth R. Maddigan.)

Paths Along Onset Bay, Mass.

Leisurely walks along the bluffs overlooking the bay contented early-20th-century visitors to Onset, like the 1920s strollers seen here, and remained fashionable for many years. Post–World War II guests of the large Onset hotels, however, sought more sophisticated diversions, and with the loss of numerous trees to hurricanes between 1938 and 1954, pleasurable walks along the bluffs became passé.

19

The Hotel Onset was Onset's first hotel, constructed by the Onset Bay Grove Association as the 19-room Prospect Park House on Onset Avenue. Renamed in 1884 as Hotel Onset, the operation was sold by the association in 1886 to New York tea merchant James B. Clark. Clark physically expanded the building for the following season and improved the grounds with swings as well as tennis and croquet courts.

HOTEL ONSET
Directly on the Waterfront
Onset, Mass.

By 1928, a total of 18 hotels were operating at Wareham, 14 of which were located at Onset, with a 15th (the Pine Tree Inn) at Point Independence. Following World War II, when modern resorts and attractions developed on Cape Cod, the Onset hotels found themselves unable to compete. In 1986, the former 55-room Hotel Onset was converted to 16 condominiums and is now known as Bayside Onset.

Electric street railways were instrumental in the growth of Onset as a resort community. The *Boston Globe* reported in June 1902: "owing to the advent of the electric car service there are more people in Onset today than ever before." Trolleys from Brockton, Middleborough, and New Bedford ran along Onset Avenue (seen here east of the Hotel Onset) and continued to Buzzards Bay.

The New Bedford & Onset Street Railway had the advantage of being able to bring guests directly to the doors of their hotels. Tracks ran atop the bluffs, passing both the Hotel Onset and Glen Cove House. Service on the street railway was never profitable, however, and it ended in 1927 due to competition from the automobile.

Built in 1883 by Nelson Huckins Sr. of Brockton, the Glen Cove House was described as the most finely furnished hotel at Onset at the time: "The Glen Cove House, occupying a sightly position on the high bluff at the end of the South Boulevard [now Onset Avenue], and overlooking the bay, is as well known to Brocktonians as is its genial proprietor, Mr. Nelson Huckins."

The hotel, with its commanding position above the bluffs, was leased to various parties to run, including Charlotte A. Ring and Mrs. A.R. Williams, who managed the property jointly, and Charles A. Neal. Huckins owned the hotel until his death in 1899, making improvements such as granite sidewalk curbing in 1888.

In 1900 and 1901, the hotel was the centerpiece of a titillating scandal when Susan E. Howard claimed Huckins's estate as his sole legitimate child. Earlier, Huckins had deserted Howard's mother, Martha, going to Iowa where he fathered several children with Martha's sister. Howard only learned these details when she mistakenly opened a letter intended for her mother years later. Her efforts to claim the hotel failed. (Courtesy of Kenneth R. Maddigan.)

The Glen Cove House remained under Huckins family ownership until 1921, when it was sold to the Helides family of Taunton. In a 1940s effort to update the hotel, a cocktail lounge addition was built overlooking the bay. Here, dancing to the Neptune Orchestra was featured in 1946. Given the shortness of the season, Onset's remaining hotels like the Glen Cove House and Hotel Onset found modernization unfeasible in the postwar era.

When summer traffic began to congest roadways to Cape Cod following World War II, the Glen Cove House advertised its "ideal location for a complete holiday vacation as well as a restful spot for a weekend." Though much outdated, the 13-room Glen Cove House operated through the early 1970s before being advertised for sale for $70,000 in 1974. Today, efforts to revitalize the historic structure continue. (Courtesy of Kenneth R. Maddigan.)

Occupying the riverside were George M. Besse's fish market and a cavernous building housing the original Glen Cove Garage. These were replaced in the 1920s by new buildings that lastly housed Leroy Besse's fish market (now the Stonebridge Bar & Grill) and the marina (operated successively by Ernest E. Besse, Leroy P. Jones, and currently, Stonebridge Marina). (Courtesy of Kenneth R. Maddigan.)

In Front of the Glen Cove Hotel, Onset, Mass.

In 1882, Nelson Huckins petitioned the Massachusetts Harbor and Land Commissioners for leave to build a wharf to operate in conjunction with the Glen Cove House. Constructed shortly thereafter, the wharf stood at the base of the bluff below the hotel. Here, Huckins rented boats and operated a naphtha-powered launch. When sold in 1921, the wharf was known as Aero Wharf and included a boat railway.

Point Independence and Huckins Wharf, ONSET, Mass.

Also utilizing the wharf was Huckins's son Nelson Jr., a successful boatbuilder at Onset, whose obituary noted that a number of Huckins-built boats were never beaten in competitive racing at Onset. One of the youngest boatbuilders along Buzzards Bay, Nelson Jr. built what he believed was the first racing boat with an adjustable fin, *Pedro*, in 1898. The younger Huckins served for several years as Onset's fire chief.

In March 1900, a fire destroyed Huckins's Ocean Avenue boatbuilding shop, threatening the Glen Cove House. Lost in the fire was a boat whose decks had been oiled the day before, ropes and fittings for a yawl, and a sloop. "The almost irremedial damage is the destruction of models and patterns which were the accumulated results of years of experience," one newspaper noted. Huckins soon rebuilt the business. (Courtesy of Kenneth R. Maddigan.)

Besides the wharf, a semiprivate beach, which included bathhouses and a private float, operated in connection with the Glen Cove House for years. As late as the 1940s, the hotel was still advertising this feature. "Glen Cove offers a private beach for bathing, providing umbrellas and beach chairs for guests as well as fresh water showers," ran one advertisement from 1947.

Two

ONSET BEACH

See Onset, Mass.
Scientific
Swimming
School
Safe
Sanitary
Sun warmed water.

From the outset, the principal attraction of Onset was its white sandy beach arcing around the bay below the bluffs. Early visitors were content with timidly wading into the warm ocean waters, but later individuals sought more active pursuits. By the 1920s, swim meets, diving exhibitions, lifesaving instruction, and drills, as well as beachside calisthenics, had become part of the summertime program at Onset Beach. (Courtesy of Kenneth R. Maddigan.)

Bathing in the sea was one of the earliest pastimes at Onset, where the beach was noted for its clean sand, relatively shallow depth, gradually descending bottom, and water that was claimed to be 10 degrees warmer than elsewhere along the Massachusetts coast. Reports of the period emphasized the warmth of the water with one in July 1908 indicating that it was "almost too warm for invigorating bathing."

Warm weather in July 1905 similarly brought out a large number of bathers, and it was noted that the water was two to five degrees warmer than the air at midday. This apparently was not one of those days, however, as the large crowd of well-dressed spectators seems content to sit on the bathhouse steps and observe the lone bather.

View of Shore, Onset, Mass.

Onset, like many Buzzards Bay communities, was noted for its lack of surf, which made it suitable for children like those seen here about 1910. The *New York Times* in 1891 had commended this feature, writing: "There is no surf, to be sure, but there is an amount of comfort to be obtained in the still-water bathing that amply compensates for the excitement that gives surf bathing its great charm."

BATHING SCENE SHOWING WICKETS ISLAND, ONSET, MASS.

Initially, the season for bathing appears to have corresponded with the start of the annual summer camp meeting in July, but it increasingly was moved forward. In June 1905, it was reported that the public bathhouses and bathing float were already in use at a time earlier than ever before. Warm weather at the time fostered an appreciation for the facilities Onset offered. (Courtesy of Kenneth R. Maddigan.)

Grove, Wharf & Shore from Shell Point, Onset, Mass.

The fine clean sand for which Onset Bay was noted and which attracted bathers to its waters served another less well-known purpose. In 1885, Capt. Joseph H. Burgess shipped large quantities of sand harvested from about the bay and the upper portion of Buzzards Bay by schooner to Taunton, Providence, and other cities, where it was used as moulding sand in metal foundries.

Through World War I, much of Onset Beach had been left in its natural state, which included beach grass and rocks on the shore and partially submerged eelgrass. Under the guidance of local organizations and the efforts of local merchant George Kashimura, the beach was subsequently improved. Poles that had formerly served as ties for skiffs were removed, grass was uprooted by hand, and new floats were installed.

ALONG THE BAY AT ONSET BAY. MASS

Improvement efforts during the 1920s affected local clam diggers. "An unpleasant situation to bathers is brought about by clam digging on the main Onset bathing beach," reported the Wareham Park Commission in 1924. As a result, clamming on public beaches was banned seasonally so that the sands might remain undisturbed and discarded clam shells would not pose a hazard to bare feet.

SHORE VIEW, ONSET, MASS.

Following its physical upgrade, Onset Beach became the venue for several organized water-related events and activities, which drew large crowds through the subsequent two decades. Postcards published by Kashimura during the era (two of which are reproduced on pages 27 and 34) cleverly employed an S monogram to advertise the safety, cleanliness, and warmth of the waters, as well as the "scientific swimming school" he was instrumental in establishing.

ON THE BEACH, ONSET, MASS.

In 1923, the Onset Woman's Club, at the suggestion of Kashimura, instituted free swimming lessons, and Onset had the only free outdoor saltwater swimming school in the United States. Kashimura, a graduate, former instructor, and performer of the Mito Swimming School in Japan, served as the Onset school's first instructor. In 1925, Kashimura was succeeded by John L. Barrett of West Roxbury.

LARGEST SALT WATER FREE PUBLIC SWIMMING SCHOOL, ONSET BAY, MASS.

Here you'll find within your reach
A diving float and bathing beach
Where children play, and May and Sam
With little shovels dig the clam
Boat races, water stunts, pave the way
For a good old time at Onset Bay

During its first year, the school trained 482 children to swim. In the course of four years, some 5,000 children were taught during the daily afternoon lessons. In addition, mass games were conducted under the supervision of the local playground association. All the activities were open to the public at no charge, and thousands availed themselves of the opportunity to learn to swim or just have fun.

In 1924, a one-story lifesaving station was erected on the beach above the new municipal bathhouse. Next to it was a tall tower that was manned by a guard during bathing times. An adjoining boat shed housed a flat-bottomed boat to be used for rescues. The station was staffed by the Onset chapter of the Red Cross Life-Saving Corps, captained by Harry Freeman and later by Kashimura.

A WONDERFUL TIME BATHING, PICK ME OUT IN THE CROWD, ONSET BAY, MASS.

During 1924, twenty-two rescues from drowning were made by the Red Cross corps at Onset, while some 465 persons were provided with emergency medical treatment—primarily cuts and bruises received while swimming in the water or playing on the beach. So successful was the program that the following year Wareham appropriated $375 to extend the lifesaving work at Onset to the town's other beaches.

See Onset, Mass.
Scientific
Swimming
School
Safe
Sanitary
Sun warmed water.

Demonstrations of lifesaving skills were provided at Onset Beach to raise awareness and to generate interest in this necessary work. This also encouraged a number of local residents to become qualified as lifesavers. The emphasis upon lifesaving was also a drawing card for safety-conscious parents, and postcards were put to use touting the safety of Onset Beach.

SAFELY GUARDED, PEACEFUL ONSET BAY, MASS.

In July 1925, in a stunt designed to promote lifesaving instruction at Onset Beach, instructor John L. Barrett had himself tied to 800 pounds of stone and thrown overboard in shoal water. Later that same month, when George Kashimura tried a similar stunt weighted with an 80-pound sandbag, the stunt went awry. Barrett rescued him in front of 10,000 concerned onlookers.

In 1925, physical culture exercises were started on the beach and were popular for both participants and spectators. The following year, Red Cross commodore William Longfellow praised Onset's programs in his organization's magazine: "where the Red Cross Life Savings Corps conducts a very full program is a municipal attraction. [Visitors] get one of the fullest beach programs in the country through cooperation of various local agencies."

While these activities remained popular through the 1930s, drawing large numbers to Onset's main beach, particularly on weekends, the beach was not always crowded. This photographic postcard template produced for Curt Teich & Company captures a more leisurely summer day from the 1930s, most likely during the middle of the week when beaches were less populated.

Bathing beauty pageants on the beach were a feature of the 1920s and 1930s, including a 1925 contest held on Onset Beach as part of the American Canoe Association regatta. Swim meets were featured on the main beach as well throughout the 1930s and 1940s and drew nationally known competitors. In 1934, national title holders Alice Bridges and Johnny Higgins were on hand to participate.

In 1942, with visitation off due to World War II, the Onset Bay Vacation Committee advertised heavily in periodicals, including the *New York Times*, promoting its "white sandy beach, water temp. 72°, dancing, bathing, boating, fishing, tennis, theatres, golf, excellent drinking water, large shade trees, seashore and country, [and] land locked bay."

Happy Summer Time at Bathing Beach, Onset Bay, Mass.

Another advertisement from 1942 called Onset's beach one of the finest on the Atlantic: "No dangerous surf or undertows . . . permits the most timid bather to enjoy water sports in water with a Summer temperature between 69 and 78 degrees." Seventeen years earlier, the 1925 promotional booklet *Onset the Beautiful* had similarly extolled Onset Beach: "a sandy beach, gently sloping, with no breakers or undertow, makes safe bathing for all."

Good Old Summertime at Onset, Mass.

July 1942 featured a two-day water carnival sponsored by the chamber of commerce with swimming races, a water ballet, exhibition diving, a bathing beauty contest (winner to be crowned Miss Camp Edwards), and 10 swimming races, including New England championship races and the national junior 50-meter freestyle. Wartime austerity and rationing, however, greatly curtailed automobile excursions after 1942, and Onset remained quiet for the remainder of the war.

44900

Efforts were undertaken by the Onset Chamber of Commerce during the postwar era to improve Onset's tourist amenities, and beginning in 1947, the main beach was illuminated at night by floodlights, which remained on nightly until 11:00 p.m. In addition to the local chamber of commerce, hotels, including the Wayside Inn, advertised the floodlit beach hoping to lure postwar visitors.

In 1955, a beach improvement committee was established for all Wareham beaches, including Onset. Onset continued to be promoted through the 1950s and 1960s as "this Summer playground, with its landlocked harbor, four picturesque islands, large modern pier and shady parks bordering the beaches [offering] an atmosphere of the country as well as seashore, for in some sections the trees grow virtually to the water's edge."

The Bathers, Onset Bay, Mass.

One attraction of the main beach at Onset was its floats. Recreational floats were present by 1887, when the Onset Bay Grove Association was granted a license to construct a floating wharf. The floats became a focal point for swimmers, and their use may have been encouraged after a 17-year-old boy diving off the wharf broke his neck in 1912. (Courtesy of Kenneth R. Maddigan.)

BATHING AT ONSET, MASS.

Initially, the floats were simple affairs consisting of a floating platform with two half walls. In time, the floats saw the addition of slides and diving platforms. Later residents recall that the slides worked well when wet but otherwise were not the most practical or enjoyable feature, particularly after having been in the hot sun for a long period of time.

Slide into Onset Bay, Mass.

The tall wooden stands of the slides were also used for diving, a channel being dug behind the floats in order to permit safe diving from the wooden platforms. The floats were the site of a diving exhibition by the Red Cross Life-Saving Corps held as part of the 1922 Knights of Pythias water carnival. Twenty years later, a similar diving display was a feature of the 1942 water carnival.

PUBLIC FLOAT AT ONSET BAY, MASS.   108745

During the disastrous 1938 hurricane, the flood tide broke one of the floats free of its moorings and carried it to the campground of the Reorganized Church of Jesus Christ of Latter-day Saints on the west side of Muddy Cove. The following year, it was refloated under the Dummy and Point Independence Bridges and put back into service at the main bathing beach.

PUBLIC BATH HOUSES, BAY VIEW GROVE, ONSET, MASS.

To accommodate bathers, numerous bathhouses were constructed, including those pictured here, which are believed to be the block that was constructed in 1897. Situated directly below Bay View Grove, they featured wooden stairs allowing bathers to easily descend into the water. The stairs also provided a convenient spot for spectators to observe the goings-on in the bay. The seawall dates from 1896, at which time the bluff was graded.

SOUTH BOULEVARD BEACH, ONSET, MASS.

The original bathhouses were constructed on an ad hoc basis. In 1912, the Onset Board of Trade was calling for the replacement of these individual bathhouses with one large central facility to be staffed by an attendant and to include "proper sanitary arrangements," arguing that such a structure would permit greater numbers of visitors to enjoy the bathing.

The matter of consolidating the private bathhouses seems to have partially resolved itself on the afternoon of March 31, 1915, when fire destroyed five bathhouses belonging to the Marcy House hotel, along with two others and a boathouse. In 1924, all remaining private bathhouses between Shell Point and the Onset wharf were removed and operations centralized in a single facility that included a roof-top dance pavilion, tables, and benches.

The capacity of the new central bathhouse, then known as the Onset Bathing Pavilion, was doubled in 1924 to accommodate 1,000 bathers. "One thousand bathers can now be given beautiful woolen suits, comfortable dressing rooms and large Turkish towels. It is a sanitary, well-appointed bathhouse, conveniently located at the edge of the bluff," read the advertising by proprietor J.L. Tuttle. (Courtesy of Kenneth R. Maddigan.)

Besides the functional purpose it served, the municipal bathhouse also featured a rooftop pavilion that was popular for dancing. Many came, however, simply to occupy a bench and enjoy the view over Onset Bay. The bathhouse was destroyed in the September 1938 hurricane when the storm tide washed over it. It was replaced, but not before an intrepid photographer captured this image of its collapsed ruins.

Following the 1938 hurricane, the bathhouse was rebuilt in 1939 with the lifesaving station incorporated into one end and the concessions at the other with a covered pavilion on the roof. At the time, the former lifesaving station was removed from the beach and put to use elsewhere as a tool shed. Since that time, the new bathhouse has continued to regularly serve summer beachgoers.

Onset lacked the formality that characterized other resorts where social conventions remained rigidly enforced. "At Onset Bay camp ground a man may walk the entire length of Onset avenue, the principal thoroughfare and only business street of any importance, attired in nothing more than an ordinary bathing suit, and he excites no comment. A man with a silk hat and kid gloves will attract more attention."

NOTHING DOING.

At Onset, Mass.

In 1897, Onset was awaiting arrival of the equally unconventional "wrapper woman," a class of women who went bathing clad only in calico gowns. "A calico wrapper when dry is a modest garb, but when wet it affords studies of 'the altogether' that enliven even the dullest season." Unsurprisingly, women eschewing suits like the ones pictured here chose to bathe at more secluded locations like Shell Point and East Boulevard.

Bathing costumes at Onset historically were a much-considered topic by newspapers. The *Boston Globe* seemed relieved in 1895 that "at last Onset boasts of a lady visitor who bathes in a fully up-to-date suit that looked as well on [the] wearer after the bath as before it was wet." The newspaper modestly approved the fact that the woolen suit when wet "refused to cling to the well-made form beneath it."

A woolen bathing suit rented at Holmes Casino, as well as use of the bathhouse on the bluffs below, could all be had for a quarter during the early 1900s, as advertised on one of the beach floats. Many chose instead to change in parked cars or went about dressed in their swimwear, much to the distress of conservative Onset residents and Wareham police. (Courtesy of Kenneth R. Maddigan.)

The Beach and Independence Point, Onset, Mass.

Promenading in one's bathing suit was a long-standing practice at Onset. The habit was noted as early as 1896, when the *Boston Globe* remarked on female bathers (like those seen here below the Hotel Onset) heading to the sea in dry suits and returning "back in wet and clinging ones, laughing and chatting in apparent unconsciousness." In 1923, Wareham adopted regulations prohibiting bathing suit–clad swimmers from appearing on Onset's streets.

TREES, BEACH AND WATER—NATURE'S COMBINATION

MEET THE CROWD AT ONSET BAY, MASS.

In 1930, Onset again enforced the rule forbidding bathing suits on the streets. "Until this order was posted a bathing suit was considered the proper Summer apparel in Onset for all save the most formal occasions." Though complaints prompted the ban, "critics were not so much shocked by what they saw as offended in an aesthetic sense by the spectacle of many promenaders to whom bathing suits are not becoming."

Three

ONSET PIER

Onset Bay from Bay View Grove, Onset, Mass.

In 1878, the original Onset wharf was built by the Onset Bay Grove Association for use of steamboats and accordingly was named Steamboat Wharf. Since that time, the wharf and its 1936 successor, the present Onset Pier, have been a focal point of the waterfront. This view depicts Steamboat Wharf in the background and Phillips' Landing in the foreground about 1910.

STEAMBOAT LANDING AT ONSET, MASS

As it used to look. They are fixing the wharf. So as to have it the same again. I am talking out loud. But as much as ever I can. Nella.

Though constructed to receive steamships bringing Spiritualists and day-trippers to Onset, Steamboat Wharf was also used by excursion boats like the *Martha's Vineyard*, seen here, which journeyed regularly to points along Buzzards Bay and Nantucket Sound. In 1883, the wharf was extended to provide berths for two steamers. The roofed structure on the wharf stood from 1895 until 1905 and provided cover for waiting passengers. (Courtesy of Kenneth R. Maddigan.)

Wharf from Grove, Onset, Mass.

The wharf was also used by coastal schooners carrying goods to and from Onset. Cargo delivered to Onset included lumber from Nova Scotia and bulk goods like coal. Shipments from Onset where there was no manufacturing and little agriculture consisted of goods harvested from the community's meager resources, including shellfish, sand, and gravel. Here, three tugboats likely involved in the construction of the Cape Cod Canal share the wharf.

The Pier, Bay and Shore, ONSET, Mass.

As the number of vessels using Steamboat Wharf declined in the early 1900s, it became a popular location for fishing. Anticipation of increased traffic due to the presence of the nearby Cape Cod Canal (construction of which began in 1909) prompted the commonwealth to deepen the channel to the Onset wharf. Plans at the time for creation of a commercial harbor and a harbor of refuge at Onset, however, remained unrealized.

The Pier, Onset, Mass.

In 1915, the Cape Cod and New Bedford Steamship Company petitioned for a rebuilt wharf at Onset, a year after the opening of the Cape Cod Canal fueled prospects for a Boston–Onset–New Bedford steamship service. Eventually, in 1917, Steamboat Wharf was repaired. New piles were driven, and the top was replaced. The wharf became redundant with construction of the town pier in the mid-1930s.

PUBL. BY
P.C. SMALL,

BATH HOUSES AND BLUFF, ONSET, MASS.

Private wharves soon joined the Onset Bay Grove Association's Steamboat Wharf. Most notable was the wharf seen here, later known as Phillips' Landing or Phillips' Wharf, which was used for boat rentals. Established in June 1884 by Capt. Joseph Dimmick, it was announced in newspapers at the time: "Capt. Joseph Dimmick has opened a boat bazaar at Onset Bay Grove, where he has all kinds of boats to let at all times."

Boat Landing, Onset, Mass.

Phillips' Wharf was essentially two floating stages, measuring 45 by 12 feet and 28 by 18 feet, joined together and connected to Onset Beach by a narrow 112-foot-long gangway carried just above the water. Deemed picturesque, it was more frequently photographed and depicted on postcards than was neighboring Steamboat Wharf.

64618

In 1886, G.H. Phillips of Brighton purchased the Dimmick operation. Arthur M. Phillips later conducted the business of renting rowboats and sailboats in conjunction with his boatyard at Point Independence. In 1903, Phillips advertised his float's convenient location opposite the Onset Bay Grove Association's open-air auditorium on Onset Avenue. The landing was easily distinguished by the conspicuous shed that occupied it.

A WATER VIEW, ONSET, MASS.

Swimmers also departed from Phillips' Landing. On August 23, 1900, George P. Moore and James Burgess Greene left the "small wharf" at Onset for the nearly three-mile swim to Monument Beach. Accompanied by several rowboats, launches, and sailboats, they arrived across Buzzards Bay one hour and 52 minutes later. "We didn't swim for notoriety but just to make an amateur record for this swim," Moore told the press.

Phillips' Landing was replaced by a pier authorized in 1917. Constructed by the Town of Wareham, which used water pressure to drive the piles, the newly built pier, as well as Steamboat Wharf seen behind it, attracted large numbers of automobilists. Clearly, motorists had no compunction about parking on public parkland, but the grading of a portion of Prospect Park in 1932 for a parking lot helped alleviate this situation.

THE PIER, ONSET, MASS.

Though no longer as heavily trafficked as it once had been, Steamboat Wharf continued to attract small sailboats and powerboats, as well as visitors eager to see them. This small crowd in the 1920s is gathered on the wharf outside Kenny's Salt Water Taffy. Straw boaters for the gentlemen and white cotton dresses for the ladies were fashionable. (Courtesy of Kenneth R. Maddigan.)

The two images on this page depict the Onset wharves in the 1920s. Produced as photographic templates by Curt Teich & Company of Chicago, a leading postcard publisher, they represent the first step of the production process whereby scenic images felt to have a wide appeal were photographed before being sent to Chicago for processing. Often, as is the case with these, the templates had a beauty of their own.

The Ellis Speed Boat Company advertised rides from the Town Pier while a competitor did the same from Steamboat Wharf. A novelty for most people in the 1920s, a ride around Onset Bay in a powerboat was an exhilarating experience. Also captured at lower right is a portion of the bathhouse roof. Visitors could climb to the roof to enjoy unimpeded views of the bay.

Town Pier, Onset Bay, Mass.

In 1936, a $68,000 steel and concrete pier replaced the earlier wooden piers and was dedicated before a crowd of 4,000 spectators on July 11. The new pier was eight times larger than the ones it replaced. Extending over 300 feet into the water, it had parking for 400 automobiles. Three-quarters of the cost was financed by the Works Progress Administration, with the balance coming from the Town of Wareham.

214—Town Parking Pier, Onset, Cape Cod, Mass.

6B-H1369

Between 1920 and 1950, the automobile transformed the way Americans vacationed, and resort areas like Onset benefitted greatly, drawing a larger number of visitors from a wider area. Businesses, including restaurants, hotels, and boardinghouses, flourished, giving Onset a renewed vibrancy and economic vitality. To accommodate the large number of automobiles arriving each summer, parking was provided regularly on the new Onset Pier beginning in the 1940s.

Onset's popularity as a destination for vacationers during the 1930s and 1940s is attested to by the large number of automobiles parked on the pier seen from Bay View Grove. Summer automobile traffic in the community during the interwar period was described as "bumper to bumper." Ironically, the automobile would also contribute to Onset's decline, with traffic on Routes 6, 28, and 25 bypassing the village beginning in the 1950s.

ONSET BEACH, ONSET, MASS.

Located at the end of the pier is an unusual octagonal building that serves as the Onset harbormaster's office. The pier retains its historic connection to excursion boats. Boat trips from the location are still available today. Both charter trips as well as regularly scheduled cruises along the Cape Cod Canal have departed the pier here for many years.

Constructed in 1895 to replace the Bay View Café, which stood directly over the water, this small building housed a fish market and, in 1903, Hyram Bryant and Joseph P. Kenny's popcorn stand, which became widely known for its many flavors of saltwater taffy. Conveniently located at the end of Steamboat Wharf and operating from the same site for over a century, Kenny's was an Onset landmark.

During the 1938 hurricane, Kenny's stand was washed from its foundations. Returned to its site, Kenny's continued to manufacture and sell the perennial summer seashore treat, as well as fudge and popcorn, later expanding to include a snack bar as part of its operation. The iconic business closed in 2011. The building, which is the sole commercial structure permitted on the beach now, houses Stash's Onset Beach restaurant.

Four

WICKET'S ISLAND

Wicket's Island has long been considered a landmark in Onset Bay; visually, it was one of the most frequently documented Onset locations on postcards. *Boston Globe* correspondent Frank P. Sibley wrote of mound-like Wicket's in 1909 when it featured a large mansion at its peak and served as a backdrop for catboats, that the island looked "as if it were imported from the Rhine." (Courtesy of Kenneth R. Maddigan.)

Wickets Island from The Bluff, Onset, Mass.

The early history of Wicket's Island is murky. In 1724, natives Nathan and Deborah Wicket devised "a certain island in a bay called Buzzards Bay . . . called Sagamore's Island" to their son Jabez and son-in-law Joseph Joseph in return for material support they received. Though Wicket's Island was noted for its absence of swampy and low-lying ground, lack of fresh water deterred settlement, and Jabez Wicket resided near Herring Pond at Plymouth.

Wickett's Island, Onset Bay, Mass.

Following Wicket's death, the town continued to recognize native rights in the island, and members of the native Webquish family owned it. According to Wareham historian Daisy Lovell, the Great Gale of 1815 eroded a portion of the island containing native burials, which washed into the sea. In 1828, the Town of Wareham conveyed the island to Hezekiah Freeman, and it subsequently came into the possession of the Hammond family.

In 1882, Dr. Abbie Cutter, a Spiritualist and "eclectic physician," opened a Spiritual Institute and Home for the infirm on the island, advertising: "Hundreds of people have of late visited this novel institution and pronounced it one of the loveliest localities in this section." While Wicket's Island offered standard tourist activities like fishing, boating, and bathing, more unusual were the séances held in the Cutter mansion. (Courtesy of Kenneth R. Maddigan.)

In 1882, Cutter advertised in the Spiritualist journal *Mind and Matter*: "To the pleasure seeker this Island offers peculiar advantages [including] delightful scenery, boating and fishing. For those with physical infirmities, every means that spirits or mortals can devise for the speedy relief and permanent cure of all will be employed. Electricity, magnetism, medicated vapor and salt-water baths, manipulations, gymnastics, with kindest care, will all be afforded to health seekers."

From the tower of the Cutter home, views could be had in all directions. This one of Point Independence was featured on a unique oblong postcard. A decade following Abbie Cutter's 1888 death, the island was purchased as a summer home by attorney Richard Ela and his brother Dr. Walter Ela of Cambridge. In 1925, Dr. F.W. Murdock of Brockton acquired the island, which included the large wooden dwelling house and other buildings from the Ela family. Some critics

at the time found the purchase price of $25,000 exorbitant, including one old-timer who recalled that "a former owner . . . would have accepted 25 cents and a pair of forward wheels for it." The old-timer would have been shocked to know that the island was offered for sale in 1985 for $4 million. (Courtesy of Kenneth R. Maddigan.)

WICKETS ISLAND, ONSET BAY.

During Prohibition, Wicket's Island is believed to have been used by rumrunners to hide liquor. The island was bought in 1959 by Harold Pilon, who restored the Cutter House after several years of abandonment, using it as a summer retreat for his family. By the 1970s, the house was no longer used regularly, and it fell prey to vandalism. It eventually burned, leaving two decayed cottages on the island.

WICKET ISLAND AND BAY, ONSET, MASS.

Wicket's Island was again offered for sale in 1990 for $3.4 million, at which time it was described by the *Boston Globe* as "maybe the most expensive cellar hole on the market." Plans today call for the permanent preservation of the island as a resource for outdoor recreation and environmental education by the Buzzards Bay Coalition with the support of the Town of Wareham.

Five

ONSET BAY

View from the Bluffs, Onset, Mass.

Onset Bay was a popular attraction, second only to the main beach. Various craft plied the waters, including rowboats, skiffs, catboats, yachts, coastal freighting schooners, steam launches, and large side-wheel steamships. Though the bay in summer was often crowded with boats and ships, in other seasons, as in this early 1900s view, it could be serenely quiet.

Outward Bound from Onset Bay, Mass.

The steamer *Martha's Vineyard* was the successor to earlier steamers, including *Monohansett* and *Island Home*, that had operated between Onset and points along Buzzards Bay and Nantucket Sound. Like its predecessors, *Martha's Vineyard*, seen here at Steamboat Wharf at Onset, made excursions that were frequently accompanied by band music. Onset vacationers visited destinations on the vessel's namesake island, including Cottage City and the colored cliffs at Aquinnah (Gay Head).

HOME AGAIN TO ONSET BAY, MASS.

The shallowness of Onset Bay troubled steamer captains and encouraged construction of a second steamboat wharf at Point Independence. Grounded twice in one week in July 1896, the excursion steamer *Martha's Vineyard* temporarily grounded in the bay again in July 1898 though only lightly loaded. "It is almost impossible for the *Martha's Vineyard* to come into the bay at low tide without getting stuck," lamented one newspaper at the time.

THE "GENEVEIVE," ONSET BAY. Issued by Holmes' Casino, Onset, Mass.

Smaller steam launches also operated, including Capt. Joseph H. Burgess's *Genevieve*, built in 1895 by J.S. Hathaway at New Bedford. Named for Burgess's wife, *Genevieve* was launched July 3 following a christening by Burgess's daughter Ethel with a bottle of Apollinaris water. The launch did service between Onset, Gray Gables, Monument Beach, Cataumet, and North Falmouth, where Burgess acquired the wharf privilege in the summer of 1897. (Courtesy of Kenneth R. Maddigan.)

On the Shore, Onset Bay, Mass.

Rowboats and skiffs could be rented from various parties along the shore and provided hours of leisure. Larger boats could also be chartered. In 1906, Arthur J. Record's auxiliary catboat *Clyto* was available for cruising, fishing, and sailing parties, while the following year, Capt. Ellwood W. Hallett similarly advertised his auxiliary sloop yacht *Shining Star*. (Courtesy of Kenneth R. Maddigan.)

Small sailboats took to the waters of Onset Bay, composing a picturesque scene for observers on the bluffs above. This view from in front of the Onset Hotel captures Onset Island to the left, Wicket's Island to the right, and between them on the horizon, Hog Island. Shortly after this image was produced, work began on dredging the Cape Cod Canal behind Hog Island.

An 1891 *New York Times* item noted the popularity of sailing at Onset as viewed from Pres. Grover Cleveland's summer home across Buzzards Bay: "Onset Bay [is] a pretty little harbor that sets back a mile to Onset . . . The Onset fleet of sailboats is large and active, and on pleasant days it dots the western horizon with dripping and darting craft that impart a comfortable suggestion of neighborly occupation."

Yacht racing became popular, and a regatta was held at Onset as early as 1875. Racing, observed from the bluffs in Onset Bay, made for an enjoyable afternoon for participants and spectators alike. Most favored of the racing yachts at Onset was the Buzzards Bay catboat, a centerboard, mainsail-only boat that handled well in rough, choppy seas. Common vessels locally, catboats had originally been used for fishing and transport.

ONSET BAY, FROM SHELL POINT, gives a good view of the harbor, with the numerous pleasure boats which make summer life enjoyable. The sail-boat at the right is the "Spray," in which the owner, Capt. Slocumb, made several trips around the world.

Racing remained popular through World War II, with regattas being held periodically. As part of the 1939 regatta, outer Onset Bay and Onset Island were encircled in red lights, a forerunner of today's Illumination Night. Cruises were also well patronized. In 1903, the yacht *Tidy Adly* made daily trips down Onset Bay, passing all points of interest. The cost was a quarter. Moonlight excursions on the bay found equal favor.

Large schools of bluefish that ran in late spring attracted sport fishermen to the waters of both Onset and Buzzards Bays. While large yachts could be chartered by well-to-do sportsmen, middle class visitors could enjoy the pastime in smaller oceangoing skiffs. Here, two young boys take part in the sport, being rewarded with a large specimen seen in the stern of their boat.

A 1911 promotional brochure published by the New York, New Haven & Hartford Railroad promoting the Buzzards Bay resorts asked, "Can you imagine the joy of cruising in a catboat over the sparkling waters of the bay with a trolling line out for bluefish? When the 'blues' are running, then does the heart of the real fisherman exult. Get out your tackle and prepare to enjoy some lively sport."

Powerboats became popular following 1900, and the bay became thick with them. More than 50 were reported as being present during the summer of 1907 in Onset Bay. The year 1908 was the first time that powerboats were raced at Onset, with a series of races being held in the bay. Powerboat racing at Onset peaked in the 1920s and early 1930s and was encouraged by organizations like the New England Outboard Association.

Spectators watched powerboat racing from Onset Pier and the bluffs. One of the most successful local racers was Onset fire chief Clayton Bishop, who won the 130-mile outboard motorboat race on the Hudson River from Albany to New York City three times. The *New York Times* described the chief as "Clayton Bishop, who fights fires from Mondays to Fridays . . . but who spends his week-ends afloat in frail little speeding cockleshells."

Powerboats served another purpose. Tradition holds that Onset Bay was active as a location for rum-running during Prohibition, as local boat owners took advantage of the shelter that Onset afforded. Scallopers and local fishermen are also believed to have traveled regularly through the Cape Cod Canal into international waters where the transfer of liquor took place, returning to Onset and other Buzzards Bay communities with their illicit cargo.

Police regularly patrolled shores along Onset Bay in search of liquor. In the summer of 1926, when the Nova Scotian schooner *Margery Austin* (resembling the one pictured here) grounded in the bay, she was searched for contraband Canadian liquor. Only a cargo of lumber was found. Years later, scallopers dredged up cases of liquor from Onset Bay, presumably heaved overboard by bootleggers pursued by the Coast Guard. (Courtesy of Kenneth R. Maddigan.)

PART OF ONSET BAY, showing a portion of the pleasure boats that make the Bay their harbor.

Shipwrecks were rare in Onset Bay, though not unknown. On November 29, 1911, the schooner *Altana M. Jagger*, with a load of gravel bound for New York, struck a rock and immediately sank, having just left the Onset wharf. Her crew managed to launch a boat and escape the suction the sinking ship created.

Hog Island by Moonlight, Onset Bay, Mass.

On March 25, 1887, the two-masted schooner *Stoney Brook*, with a cargo of Onset sand destined for Connecticut, ran aground on a ledge in Hog Island Narrows immediately outside Onset Bay. The crew landed on the island, but the fate of the ship is unknown. It is supposed that she remained grounded and eventually broke apart.

Even rarer sights were witnessed on Onset Bay, including a solar eclipse in September 1905. The *Boston Post* reported at the time: "It is said that D[avid] T. Burrell, an Onset photographer, got a scoop on Harvard professors by getting a photo of the recent eclipse of the sun. Undoubtedly the enthusiasts who were unfortunate in not being eyewitnesses would appreciate an opportunity of seeing it on paper."

More alarming were the 1907 forest fires in western Barnstable County. One fire threatened to destroy nearby Bourne village, and the smoke from it, which towered on the eastern horizon, was captured by a photographer on August 19 from Onset Bay. The following day, the wind shifted and the fire changed direction, rapidly advancing towards South Sandwich, Forestdale, Mashpee, and Pocasset on the eastern shore of Buzzards Bay before being stopped.

Six

ONSET AVENUE

Main Street, Onset, Mass.

S. J. SMITH, Onset, Mass.

Onset Avenue between Union Avenue and Flagstaff Square developed as Onset's commercial district, catering largely to summer residents. By 1903, about the time this picture was taken, crowded Onset Avenue and its immediate vicinity was the location of half of Wareham's restaurants, eight of its 11 hotels, four of its five bakeries, both its photographers, and all its express agencies and art supply dealers. (Courtesy of Kenneth R. Maddigan.)

The commercialized portion of Onset Avenue began at Union Avenue. Though cottages had originally been built facing Onset Avenue, many were converted to use as restaurants and stores. George W. Manning and Benjamin E. Tabor operated a bakery (later conducted solely by Manning) at the corner of Onset Avenue and South Boulevard. (Courtesy of Kenneth R. Maddigan.)

Across Onset Avenue was Edward J. Jones's Onset Souvenir Corner (right), which in 1910 sold postcards and Indian goods. Fred Eldridge operated a similar variety store at Onset and East Central Avenues, advertising a "full line of 5 and 10 cent goods, Fishing Tackle, Toys, Books, Tinware, Glass-ware, in fact everything you need, Milk, Butter and Groceries."

Onset Avenue, Onset, Mass.

In the 1920s, the Onset Souvenir Corner building housed Whitehead's Pharmacy, "Headquarters for the Vacationists." Drugs, sundries, toilet articles, cigars, soda, candy, and, of course, picture postcards were all sold. Presently the building is occupied by the popular Pier View Restaurant. Beyond the Onset Souvenir Corner on Onset Avenue in this view is the four-story Hotel Brockton.

Onset Avenue, Onset Bay, Mass.

In the generation between this image and that on page 74, the south side of Onset Avenue (on the left in both images) had been replaced by more substantial business blocks. The building on the immediate left (now Marc Anthony's) housed William Freeman's Department Store, which advertised itself as an alternative to crowded city shops. The building still retains its impressive stamped tin ceiling.

In 1885, the 20-room Union Villa on Union Avenue was built by Frank Union and featured a dining room as well as private bathrooms. Ten years later under proprietor Henry Wheelwright Lewis, it was described as "one of the prettiest, neatest and most home-like hotels in Onset. Although an invalid, Mr. Lewis has general oversight over the whole establishment, and [it] has been crowded with guests all summer."

In 1896, electric call bells and fire escapes were added for the convenience and safety of guests. The dining room where ice cream and a 50¢ fish and meat shore dinner were served was promoted as "the coolest in Onset." Nearby Macy's Oriental Store, established in 1885, advertised "the best assortment of Souvenirs and Beach Novelties." The former Union Villa now houses the offices of the Onset Bay Association.

Hotel Brockton was built on Onset Avenue just west of Union Avenue for the 1884 season and was conducted by Benjamin J. Keith of the hotel's namesake city. In May 1885, plans to increase its size and improve its appearance were announced, and it quickly rivaled the larger older hotels. In 1922, it was restyled as the New Hotel Brockton. It survives, though altered, as apartments. (Courtesy of Kenneth R. Maddigan.)

Hotel Brockton,
ONSET, MASS.

Onset Ave. showing New Onset Theatre,
Onset, Mass.

Movies came to Onset in 1907 when the first movie house was built. In addition to the Onset (later the New Onset) Theatre on the north side of Onset Avenue between Union and Highland Avenues, pictured here, there was the Pastime with its elaborate entrance advertising "Refined Entertainment for Man, Woman and Child" on Union Street and the Colonial Theatre on Onset Avenue at Tenth Street.

(Photo by Hicks)

Looking west along Onset Avenue, the Bertino Block (left) housed the Onset Gift Shop and other businesses. The three-story building with bay windows on the right was the home of Benjamin W. Iris's drugstore, which was known for its famous sodas and frappes. The marquee for the New Onset Theatre is visible at the far right above the car.

Onset Avenue, Onset Bay, Mass.

A view in the opposite direction shows Onset Avenue looking east with Highland Avenue on the left. In 1903, A.F. Farwell, confectioner, had a store at the corner of Onset and Highland Avenues and was noted for "Onset Pop Corn" and all varieties of saltwater taffy. Homemade candy and potato chips were made fresh daily.

Just off Onset Avenue, the Marcy House on Prospect Avenue was established in the late 1800s as a hotel by Charles D. Marcy of Boston. It included a dining room sufficiently large to host numerous functions over the years and operated year-round. Beginning in 1934, the 30-room hotel was conducted as the New Prospect Inn. Though the hotel closed long ago, the building survives.

One block west was Mrs. Ronald's Lunch Room and Restaurant established about 1892 in a small Pleasant Avenue cottage by John A. and Rose N. Ronald. Ronald's featured five-course dinners with ice cream for 40¢. Open 6:00 a.m. to 9:00 p.m., the restaurant's planked fish and sirloin steak were specialties. "The place has a high reputation among the best people that frequent Onset," read a 1903 advertisement.

Flag Staff Square, Onset, Mass.

Known as Flagstaff Square from the flagpole that once graced the site, this central green space at Onset and West Central Avenues was the terminus for the Onset Bay Grove Railroad from 1885 until 1890. Informally known as the Dummy Railroad because of its use of modified or "dummied" steam locomotives, the line carried passengers from the Old Colony Railroad's main line station near present-day Main Avenue and Cranberry Highway.

Park, Onset, Mass.

Earlier known as both Central and Post Office Square, following World War II, busy Flagstaff Square was renamed for Dudley L. Brown, a local soldier killed during World War I for whom the VFW post established in 1933 is also named. Notably, the shop at the far left sold picture postcards for a nickel each, many of which appear in this volume. (Courtesy of Kenneth R. Maddigan.)

BAND CONCERT AT FLAG STAFF SQ., ONSET, MASS.

Despite its name, a flag frequently appears absent in images of Flagstaff Square. In 1916, the daily honor of raising the flag was left to those passing the square earliest each morning after constable Charles Benson abandoned the task because, alarmingly, "he continually got the flag upside down . . . Now the work of attaching the Stars and Stripes . . . is left to the first patriotic citizen who happens to stroll by," noted one newspaper.

Business Centre, Onset, Mass.

Triangular Flagstaff Square was surrounded by business blocks. The north side of the "square" seen here housed a restaurant, Kashimura's Japanese Bazaar, and an ice cream manufactory. The one-story block in the center at the corner of Onset and Highland Avenues housed the Onset Post Office and was known alternately as Bullock's Block and the Post Office Block. The Knights of Pythias later added a second-story hall.

THE SQUARE, ONSET, MASS.

In the 1920s, Onset Avenue remained a bustling commercial district, the street crowded with automobiles and the New Bedford streetcars and sidewalks congested with pedestrians. The eponymous flagpole (this time flying a flag) was still present at Flagstaff Square and remained a landmark. Young's Restaurant is visible through the trees at right.

INTERIOR, YOUNG BROS. CAFE, MAIN AND WEST CENTRAL AVENUE, ONSET, MASS.

Young Brothers opened their restaurant at Flagstaff Square in the 1910s. Restyled as Young Bros. Café, in 1919 the establishment advertised itself as suitable for ladies and gentlemen, offering chicken, steak, and lobster dinners, as well as a la carte meals at all hours. The produce and poultry served were raised on Young Brothers' own farm on Dick's Pond, which like the restaurant was advertised on a number of postcards.

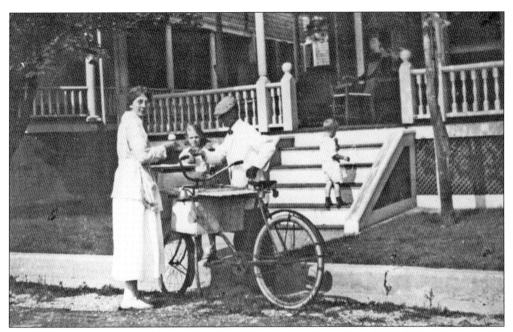

Ice cream vendors circulated throughout the village, as seen here about 1925. At the time, two ice cream parlors operated on Onset Avenue—the Puritan Ice Cream Parlor and Charles H. Waters's Onset Ice Cream Parlor. Waters also sold candy, sodas, and cigars, and according to his 1903 ad, was the "only place on the Beach that serve[d] the genuine college ice," sundaes atop a layer of crushed ice.

Outgrowing its Pleasant Avenue location, John A. Ronald's Ronald Inn and Café relocated to West Central Avenue near Flagstaff Square about 1910. Ronald's proclaimed itself "Famous for its table d'hôte dinners and service a la carte." Seafood, according to another advertisement, was a specialty. Two hundred diners could be accommodated in the dining room while additional space was provided by the screened open-air pavilion.

THE RONALD INN, ONSET, MASS

Unlike many other Onset businesses that operated seasonally, the Ronald Inn and Café was open year-round, building a loyal local clientele in addition to its out-of-town patrons. For years, Ronald's advertised heavily by a number of means, publishing postcards like these as well as placing advertisements in the popular *Automobile Blue Book* and *Green Book* guides of the day.

THE RONALD INN, ONSET, MASS.

While central Onset is remembered for the devastating gas main explosion of 1946, a previous smaller explosion at the Ronald Inn and Café in November 1925 claimed the life of employee and boarder John R. Barrows, who was engaged in changing a tube on a gas pressure device. The subsequent fire spread to a neighboring home, though the inn was left untouched.

Main Dining Room,   The Ronald Inn,   Onset, Mass.

Despite the fact that the Ronald Inn and Café attracted the "finest clientele," it was a victim of declining patronage during World War II, when many food items were rationed and automobile usage restricted. In 1942, the inn, including the restaurant and six guest rooms, was offered for sale. The former restaurant building still stands at 4 West Central Avenue.

On July 18, 1946, nine were killed when a ruptured gas main exploded at Christy's Spa (the building just left of center). Sixty individuals were injured by flying glass and debris while others were buried beneath the remains of four collapsed wood-frame buildings. "Eyewitnesses reported some victims were blown bodily from the buildings into Onset Avenue," reported one local paper. "Concussion tossed plates and utensils to the ceiling in a restaurant 250 feet" away.

The casualties that day were William English, proprietor of Christy's Spa; Gaetano "Guy" Rizzutto, owner of the fish and chips shop who subsequently died at St. Luke's Hospital, Middleborough; Catherine Rizzutto, his wife; Amy Baker Heald, Onset; Joanna Rose, Onset; Cecil Barrett, Onset; Elizabeth Mae Ward, New Bedford; Frank Albrecht, Somerville; and Raymond F. Brune, Sandwich. (Courtesy of Kenneth R. Maddigan.)

Wareham declared a state of emergency as crews from neighboring towns responded and the last victim was drawn from the wreckage some nine hours after the noontime blast. Plymouth Superior Court subsequently cited plumber Cecil Barrett, who died in the explosion, of carelessness in accidentally breaking the pipe and igniting the gas, and faulted the Buzzards Bay Gas Company for failing to have men ready to respond to such emergencies.

Seven

AROUND ONSET

Glimpse of South Boulevard looking East, Onset, Mass.

South, East, North and West Boulevards were built as part of the original 1870s layout of Onset Bay Grove. Running about the perimeter of the camp meeting grounds, the roadways were intended to provide opportunities for strolling and scenic carriage drives. Encompassed within them were a number of sites both scenic and curious.

The Road to Jordan, Onset Bay, Mass.

Most attractive of all the roadways was tree-lined South Boulevard, which ran atop the bluffs above Onset Bay. As early as summer 1879, a 1,500-foot-long boardwalk was constructed on South Boulevard prior to camp meeting, and building continued thereafter. South Boulevard's plank, and later asphalted, walkway was ideal for promenading, and it drew casual strollers who came to admire the views.

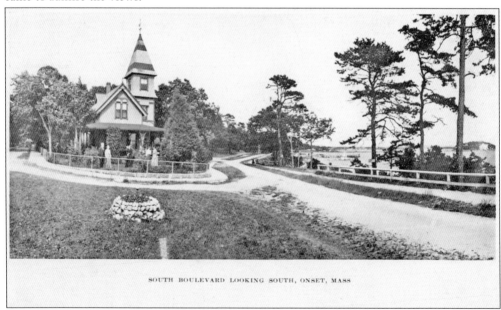

SOUTH BOULEVARD LOOKING SOUTH, ONSET, MASS

South Boulevard's crushed oyster shell–covered roadbed also invited cycling, particularly in the morning before the heat of the day. In 1894 the *Boston Globe* reported, "men, women and children raised the dust on the clam shell roads from early morning till the first toot of the cornet announced the arrival of the band in the pavilion." Ten thousand bushels of oyster shells were required in 1896 to cover Onset's roads. (Courtesy of Kenneth R. Maddigan.)

South Boulevard,
looking West, Onset, Mass.

Automobiling succeeded cycling in popularity after the turn of the 20th century and became a noted diversion at Onset. Automobiles were first mentioned in 1903 with local enthusiasts T.D. Barry, L.Q. White, Howard Miller, and Will Hurley. Astute livery stable proprietors like Nathan R. Besse on Onset Avenue at Tenth Street soon started servicing and repairing automobiles.

First House Built at Onset Bay Grove, Onset, Mass.

The first Onset cottage was built May 15, 1877, on South Boulevard by Sophia S. Applin of Fitchburg. Named Bay View Cottage, it was soon joined by hundreds more. The *Boston Globe* reported in 1882: "The incessant hammering of the builders is heard throughout the village of Onset once more, to the utter disgust of those who came here from their city homes to avoid the clamor which does not 'exist' here. Oh, no!"

"The House that Jack Built",
Onset, Mass.

Typical of the cottages built during the development of Onset was The House that Jack Built. Erected sometime after 1889 when Evelyn L. Savage of Revere acquired the lot at the intersection of Longwood Avenue and West Boulevard, the house is identifiable by its unique jerkin-head dormers. The house still stands and continues to bear a plaque with its name.

Residence of Mrs. Mary C. Weston, West Central Ave.   ONSET, Mass.

Nearby was the house of Mary C. Weston, known as Ramona Cottage. A wealthy resident of Waterville, Maine, whose uncle had briefly served as governor of that state, Weston was a devoted Spiritualist instrumental in the establishment of the On-i-set Wigwam. She also encouraged Wabanaki and Mi'kmaq natives to come to Onset in the 1890s. The cottage still stands at 51 West Central Avenue.

Many Onset cottages featured small tidy gardens, though this example on West Central Avenue was unusual for both its size and the inclusion of an attractive lily pond. One 1884 visitor to Onset remarked upon the "clean, shaded grounds, rows of beautiful cottages, with their little gardens and nicely-trimmed trees." Pedestrians like the woman with the sun umbrella depicted here often stopped during their strolls to admire such private gardens.

The principal route from Flagstaff Square to Shell Point, West Central Avenue was "radically" improved for 1899, with one local correspondent reporting, "the town of Wareham has made a handsome macadam roadway out of one of the very worst residential street's sand path anywhere about this country." A decade later, the street had fine sidewalks and numerous shade trees, although the roadway itself remained a sandy stretch.

Most hotels were located near the center of Spiritualist activity at Onset, but the Washburn House on Longwood Avenue opposite Longwood Park near Shell Point was an exception. Operated by a Mr. Washburn from Brant Rock, the hotel was expanded in 1885 and did considerable business. Unlike other Onset hotels where a transient clientele stayed for a few days only, the Washburn House attracted more long-term guests.

LARGEST AND MOST ATTRACTIVE PRIVATE HOTEL BALL ROOM ON CAPE COD   RECEPTION ROOM

VERANDA

NEW LONGWOOD GARDEN HOTEL, ONSET BAY, MASS.

The Washburn House was transformed in the 1920s into the elegant Longwood Garden Hotel, which operated through World War II. The Longwood featured a ballroom, which hosted an orchestra. Hot and cold showers on all floors were advertised, as were meals on American or European plans. The hotel also included a delicatessen and bakery at the Third Street entrance, proclaiming "only food of quality found in this hotel."

Over Jordan on Great Neck opposite Onset was described in 1909 (when Frank Paige of Springfield was constructing a $10,000 villa there) as "the locality that the recently deceased Albert Shaw, landlord of the Kendrick House at Wareham Narrows, for many years, made famous as a clambake place." A typical Buzzards Bay catboat, which was popular in the waters of Onset, appears to the right.

OVER JORDAN FROM SHELL POINT, ONSET BAY, MASS

Clambakes held at Over Jordan were well noted in the 1880s and 1890s and were conducted by others besides Shaw. W.O. Cutler heavily advertised his bakes in the Boston newspapers in 1891. Adding to the picturesqueness of the site was an old wreck that was burned by local boys the night before July 4, 1896. By the time these images appeared, Over Jordan's heyday as a recreational site had passed.

Swimmers of Back Beach, Onset, Mass.

Look for Me in this Crowd.

As early as 1878, Shell Point, the southerly end of the bluffs extending into Onset Bay, was cleared and used by the public. The beach on the backside of Shell Point became known as Back Beach and was historically less crowded than the main beach at Onset, though not on the day this image was captured. Over Jordan appears in the background across Sunset Cove.

Bathers near foot of 2nd St., West Side, Onset, Mass.

Sea bathing was also available on the west side below West Boulevard. Like Onset Beach, the water here in shallow Sunset Cove was warm. The *New York Times* in 1891 noted the numerous bathing options Onset offered: "There are many shallow spots along shore, and the number of coves in which the water is exposed to the sun upon beaches that have been warmed at low tide is innumerable."

Like elsewhere in Onset, boating on Sunset Cove, seen here below West Boulevard, was popular. The rowing abilities of Onset residents were instrumental in saving numerous lives. In August 1907, Frances Lloyd, while alone on Onset Bay, rowed to the rescue of a capsized vessel, rescuing Henry Winslow of Boston and his two young children. Newspapers cited many other similar incidents over the years. (Courtesy of Kenneth R. Maddigan.)

While Sunset Cove offered a secluded location for swimming, it was also noted for private shellfish beds that were reserved for family use and barred to commercial fishermen. Beds in Sunset Cove, as well as elsewhere along the shores of Onset Bay, were periodically seeded with shellfish, and the area was well noted for its clams, quahogs, scallops, and oysters. (Courtesy of Kenneth R. Maddigan.)

Colonial Theatre Onset, Mass.

The Colonial Theatre at Onset Avenue and Tenth Street originated as a vaudeville house in 1909. Later, a two-story casino housing a 20-lane bowling alley and second-floor Nautical Ballroom was added. During the swing era, the Colonial Theatre attracted top-name acts, including Kay Kyser, Benny Goodman, Duke Ellington, Tommy Dorsey, Rudy Vallee, Harry James, Guy Lombardo, Chick Webb, and Ella Fitzgerald. Later, Fats Domino, the Platters, and Jackie Wilson performed.

Colonial Theatre and Casino, Onset, Mass.

Though the casino (pictured with the addition) once hosted top-name performers, the caliber of entertainment declined after 1946 when Ruth McGurk was found murdered in a Carver cranberry bog after having last been seen at a dance at the casino. Though a 25-year-old Onset resident was tried at the time, he was acquitted. The crime remains unsolved.

Onset Ave. Showing Casino and Colonial Theatre, Onset, Mass.

The casino was the location of a near riot on August 13, 1960, following a rock 'n' roll dance attended by 1,300. Twenty-one local police along with state troopers from three barracks were called to quell the disturbance. Eleven were arrested, and the town subsequently banned events at the venue, prompting the *Boston Globe* to trumpet "Wareham Bans Dancing, Fears Hoodlum Invasion." The casino was destroyed by arson in 1964.

Located along unappealingly named Muddy Cove some distance from the center of happenings at Onset, North Boulevard was perhaps unsurprisingly slow to develop, with only five cottages built prior to 1903. In the following decade, growth accelerated, and a number of new houses were built to take advantage of the pleasant water views. Their modest size reflected their owners' middle class origins.

THE WIGWAM,
ONSET, MASS.

The Wigwam, Onset, Mass.

One building connected with Spiritualism was the On-i-set Wigwam, built in 1894 opposite Crescent Park by the On-i-set Wigwam Co-Workers Association founded three years earlier and dedicated to the use of Native American spiritual guides. The specifications for the building were said to have been directed by native spirits. Construction of the building, which was intended to be used as a healing center, was funded largely by Mary C. Weston.

In its first year, the On-i-set Wigwam attracted over 4,000 attendants to its daily meetings where many claimed to be cured of their ailments. Since that time, the On-i-set Wigwam has remained an active institution at Onset. For its centenary in 1994, the building was restored, including re-shingling with 9,000 hand-carved cypress shingles. It is considered the only building of its kind in the world.

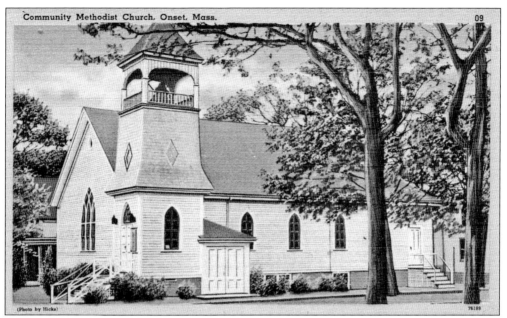

(Photo by Hicks)   76189

In 1903, the First Spiritualist Church on Highland Avenue was erected. The next year, the neighboring Methodist church was dedicated on September 4. Given the local appeal of Spiritualism, orthodox religions like Methodism had difficulty making inroads at Onset. A Methodist revival meeting conducted in 1900 was not particularly welcomed. In 1894, Onset Spiritualists opposed Clarence Stuart's bid to become postmaster. The reason? He was a Methodist.

(Photo by Hicks)   76187

For a community conducted nearly exclusively as a summer camp meeting, schools were not an early priority. Eventually, agitation by year-round Onset residents resulted in construction of a school on the reserve ground at Eleventh Street in the 1880s. The school, named in 1984 for Ethel E. Hammond, who taught second grade there for 44 years, is depicted following its $35,000 addition of two classrooms and a recreation hall in 1925.

The Temple and Arcade, Onset, Mass.

Raised in 1885 at the corner of Union Avenue and Bishop Street, the Onset Spiritualist Temple was intended for Spiritualist lectures and public séances. Construction of the temple, however, was fraught with controversy and created a lasting rift within the management of the Onset Bay Grove Association. As Spiritualism waned at Onset, use of the temple was increasingly given over to secular entertainments such as dancing, concerts, and vaudeville shows.

TEMPLE AND ARCADE, ONSET BAY, MASS.

The temple was later converted to a movie house known as the Cape Theatre, the uppermost portion of the distinctive tower having been removed. In the 1970s, the landmark building was disassembled to create a parking lot. Behind the temple on Union Avenue was the arcade building, which began life as a roller-skating rink where roller polo was popular.

Fishing from Dummy Bridge, Onset, Mass.

In 1879, the Massachusetts legislature authorized construction of a bridge to carry traffic across the narrows at Muddy Cove. Dummy Bridge took its name from the Onset Bay Grove Railroad, which employed "dummy" locomotives on its line that crossed the bridge between 1885 and 1890. Though use of the dummies was discontinued, the name stuck.

DUMMY BRIDGE, ONSET, MASS.

47275

The original Dummy Bridge was a double-span timber and steel-framed truss bridge and was once the principal means of access to Onset, carrying Main Avenue over Muddy Cove. The wooden bridge was destroyed during the 1938 hurricane and replaced the following year with this single-span steel girder bridge built by Vulcan Construction and the American Bridge Company.

The 1938 New England hurricane devastated Onset, striking September 21, 1938, at a time of day when tides were in flood. Residents of the village found refuge from successive tidal waves in the upper stories of buildings, though not everyone escaped. Eighty-year-old Archelous E. Bassett drowned while trying to swim away from his flooded home.

Those who remained on Onset Island, where 12 cottages were swept away and the remaining 30 greatly damaged, were forced to climb trees to escape the storm waves. The Prospect Inn, Methodist church, and Onset school were all used as shelters under the direction of the Welfare Department. Additionally, 130 homeless persons were sheltered at the Onset Women's Club while Marcus M. Copeland's home was used as a children's hospital.

At Riverside, three cottages were washed from their pilings, landing near Dummy Bridge, which was washed away. Automobiles stood in flooded fields while roads were so badly damaged that only narrow pathways could be opened, including Onset Avenue, which was blocked by a clutter of boats and building debris. National Guardsmen were deployed to bar sightseers from the wrecked area.

Following the 1938 hurricane, every Onset cottage except one reportedly was rebuilt. A September 1944 hurricane and two others 11 days apart in 1954 brought further damage. Though less severe than previous hurricanes, 1954's Hurricane Carol resulted in one death at Onset when the baby daughter of Mrs. Robert Crosby was swept away as Mrs. Crosby was attempting to flee rising flood waters on a cottage roof at Onset Island.

Onset's Water Supply, Sandy Pond, Onset, Mass.

Facilitating Onset's growth, municipal services were introduced, including a water supply filtered through "miles" of white sand. The Onset Water Company was formed in 1892 by Joseph K. Nye, William F. Nye, and Henry G. Dennis to furnish residents of Onset, Point Independence, and Plymouth Park with water for domestic purposes and the extinguishing of fires. It was authorized to draw from Sand Pond, mislabeled here as nearby Sandy Pond.

"Old Dummy Bridge", Onset Bay, Mass.

Conspicuous in numerous images of Dummy Bridge is the Onset Water Company's standpipe that stood in Wabun Grove. In early 1924, the company created controversy when it ceased paying rent to the Onset Bay Grove Association based on the 1916 decree that Wabun Grove was public land. The association claimed that the decree did not apply to the standpipe grounds and demanded its rental fee.

DUMMY BRIDGE, ONSET BAY.   Issued by Holmes' Casino, Onset, Mass

Hampered by low pressure within the waterworks system in quelling a $60,000 blaze on Second and Third Avenues that burned six cottages on September 21, 1920, the Onset Fire District in 1924 was authorized to purchase the Onset Water Company and maintain the water supply. The water company proposed a buyout of $85,000, but petitioners balked given the poor condition of the existing waterworks.

Slab City, Onset Bay, Mass.

A number of cottages along East Boulevard below Wabun Grove were constructed on piles over the tidewater, and the area consequently became pejoratively known as Pile City, Spile City, and Slab City. In 1913, nearby residents concerned about access to the beach and desirous of building a seawall between Glen Cove and Dummy Bridge opposed the construction of these houses. They remain to this day.

East River & North Point from East Boulevard, Onset, Mass.

Farther south along East Boulevard with no houses between the roadway and the water, delightful views were to be had across the East River towards North Water Street at Point Independence, as seen here. Though scenic, the East River historically was a working river providing access to both Muddy and Broad Coves where once productive shellfishing grounds were located.

East Boulevard, Onset, Mass.

The sandy shoreline along the East River attracted early cottage builders and bathers. Since that time, much of the shore has been built up through dredging of the East River, a process that has helped rehabilitate shellfish grounds as well as improve local beaches where the unpolluted sand was deposited.

Eight

POINT INDEPENDENCE

Residence and Beach,
Onset Bay, Mass.

Point Independence was developed on Long Neck opposite Onset as a purely commercial 227-lot subdivision by Job D. Hammond beginning in 1882. Though a distinct community from Onset and unaffiliated with Spiritualist development there, Point Independence is often considered part of Onset as a whole. The point itself is conspicuous by the tile-roofed house formerly conducted as the Point Independence Inn, which dominates the site and is visible throughout Onset.

Originally Onset and Point Independence were connected by a cable ferry, but in 1888, the Town of Wareham was authorized to build a wooden pile bridge across Swift's Narrows. Contractor for the bridge built in 1889–1890 was Earl T. Ryder of Middleborough. Material was transported to the Onset station and hauled by cart to the point. Here, the bridge is viewed from Onset's East Boulevard. (Courtesy of Kenneth R. Maddigan.)

In 1901, the Middleboro, Wareham & Buzzards Bay Street Railway received authorization to construct a second 13-foot-wide bridge adjacent to the existing highway bridge in order to carry its trolley line across the East River. The trolley encouraged further development of Point Independence and opened areas beyond Onset, including Buzzards Bay and Monument Beach, to summer day-trippers. This view is from the beach below East Boulevard.

HIGHWAY BRIDGE, ONSET BAY, MASS.

In 1914, the two bridges were replaced with a three-span reinforced concrete bridge, 271 feet long and built at a cost of $40,000. Work was delayed when the six carpenters on the job walked out following a quarrel with the superintendent in charge in March 1914. The bridge was much photographed following its completion, and its image appeared on numerous postcards.

HIGHWAY BRIDGE, ONSET, MASS.

Construction of the bridge involved disruption of the electric street railway service of the New Bedford & Onset Street Railway. Service was suspended between September 26, 1913, and June 30, 1914. The Point Independence Bridge was completed at the end of June 1914, and the first trolley crossed on July 1. It was described at the time as the "new cement arch bridge." The Glen Cove House appears at left.

Highway Bridge and Water Street,   Onset, Mass.

The Point Independence Bridge facilitated automobile travel through Onset, which also had been heavy on its predecessor. "Onset is being termed 'Autoists' Paradise' and there seems to be well founded reason for the term," noted the *Barnstable Patriot* in 1912. "No less than 3,800 autos crossed over Point Independence bridge between 9.30 a.m. and 6 p.m. Sunday July 28. Three different parties counted them and reached the same figure."

HIGHWAY BRIDGE, ONSET, MASS.

At the time of its construction in 1914, Massachusetts was noted for its program of road building, and it was remarked by one travel guide that the Point Independence Bridge "will add to the pleasure of the trip to Woods Hole." Traffic over the Point Independence Bridge continued to increase following World War I as the automobile came more widely into use, helping open the Cape to development.

THE NEW BRIDGE. ONSET. MASS

The area's excellent macadam roads, including the main route to Cape Cod from the west, which ran through Onset, were noted in travel guides of the era. Roadside filling stations were established, including the Glen Cove Garage on the Onset side of the Point Independence Bridge. The garage and seven autos were destroyed in a $30,000 fire on December 16, 1920. (Courtesy of Kenneth R. Maddigan.)

Boats on Main St Onset Mass.

During the 1938 hurricane, Onset sustained $2 million worth of damage, including a half-million worth of damage to its yachting fleet. Twenty cabin cruisers and 80 other boats were driven ashore, including the cruisers *Pustacaun* and *Pandora*, seen washed up on the Point Independence Bridge. At the bridge, the storm tide rose 11.8 feet above mean high water. National Guard troops were dispatched to prevent looting.

Like Onset, Point Independence developed a commercial district along Main Street (now Onset Avenue). Many businesses catered specifically to the summer crowd. In 1903, Lottie W. Williams conducted The Sugar Bowl, an appropriately named candy store and bakery selling all kinds of confections, cakes, pies, bread, pastry, milk, and tonic, as well as tobacco and cigars, at the corner of Third Avenue and Main Street.

Main Street, Point Independence, Onset Bay, Mass. 13

Convenient grocery stores that saved a trip into Onset were well patronized. Hammond & Smith was operating by 1897 and initially occupied the building at 157 Onset Avenue (left). Soon reorganized as Hammond & Robbins by Arthur B. Hammond and Charles A. Robbins, the new firm conducted its business at Onset Avenue and Locust Street. In the 1920s, George Lang & Company were in the grocery trade at Point Independence.

Main St., Point Independence, Mass.

In 1903, H.C. Goodspeed conducted his New Dining Room and Ice Cream Parlors, which advertised as specialties the unlikely pairing (though not served together) of oysters and ice cream. Other offerings were cigars, confectionaries, fruit in season, ice cold soda, and "temperance drinks," Onset then being a dry community. Ice cream lovers a generation later patronized Greene's, seen here.

Post Office,   Point Independence, Mass.

On March 8, 1923, True S. Hill was appointed postmaster for the new office at Point Independence, purchasing the block seen here at 146 Onset Avenue in 1927 to fill the purpose. Elizabeth C. Hall and Kenneth L. Seaver succeeded Hill, but likely due to declining wartime receipts, the post office was discontinued on June 17, 1942, and mail rerouted through Onset. (Courtesy of Kenneth R. Maddigan.)

Residential development was drawn to Point Independence, where the majority of local building in the 1890s occurred, the most desirable lots at Onset having by then been acquired. In August 1890, fifty seashore lots "beautifully shaded with pine and oak trees" were advertised at auction. The gambrel-roofed cottage in the center of this view remains at 7 North Water Street, as does the cottage to its right, though much altered.

The horse car line from East Wareham Station to the Point Independence Bridge and the street railway that succeeded it encouraged the construction of cottages; these tended to be larger than those at Onset. The large cottage at right survives at North Water and Holly Streets, though it has since lost the architectural detail seen here. The Onset Water Company's standpipe appears in the distance.

Beach & Point Independence by Moonlight, Onset, Mass

To a large extent, Point Independence was developed by Brocktonians, including Albert H. Fuller, editor of the *Brockton Enterprise*. Partially due to Fuller's influence, Brocktonians flocked to Point Independence, where nearly 100 cottages had been erected by 1895. The large number of Brocktonians summering at Point Independence led to its characterization as a "suburb" of Brockton. (Courtesy of Kenneth R. Maddigan.)

View of Onset, Mass.

While South Water Street property with its fine views towards the Onset bluffs was highly sought after as cottage lots, it served another purpose. In 1905, an experimental "clam garden" of 1,000 clams was planted on the shore near the foot of Hammond Street by the Massachusetts Fish and Game Commission with the purpose of studying the shellfish industry. Earlier stations had been established at Chatham and Wood's Hole.

Residential Section, Point Independence, Mass.

Swift's Narrows at the Point Independence Bridge was a popular bathing area. In 1893, bathing there along South Water Street was noted by the *Boston Globe* as "the great pastime here. Point Independence is crowded with visitors as never before, and they take to bathing and clambake picnics as naturally as the original Wareham settlers." Though construction of seawalls seen in this mid-1940s view shortened the beach, it continued to rival those at Onset.

SAFEST WARM WATER BATHING BEACH ON NORTH ATLANTIC COAST. POINT INDEPENDENCE. ONSET BAY. MASS.

Like Onset, Point Independence promoted the safety of its beaches. The house in the background is the Elmer E. Clapp cottage (1896), later the Point Independence Inn. At the time the house was built, the *Boston Post* reported, "Mr. Clapp has a new racing catboat, just turned out by C.C. Hawley, the Buzzard's bay builder of so many winners among the famous Cape Cod cats. It is a 27-footer."

PINE TREE INN,
ONSET, MASS.

Though a hotel was part of the original Point Independence plan, it was not until 1894–1895 that the Pine Tree Inn was built by the Point Independence Company of New York, comprised of Irving C. Hammond of Onset, Caleb S. Benson of Boston, Albert H. Fuller and Edward M. Thompson of Brockton, Edwin W. Hammer of Newark, William J. Jenks of New York City, and William H. Lanman of Brooklyn.

Pine Tree Inn, Point Independence from Island Wharf, Onset, Mass.

Advertising itself as the "coolest spot on the coast," the Pine Tree Inn was immediately popular. By 1898, it had emerged (according to the *Boston Post*) as "the most popular house on the upper shore of [Buzzards] Bay." Managed at the time by Albert Shaw, so great was the demand for rooms there that the hotel had turned away prospective guests; that August, it was characterized as being "crowded to the doors."

Island Wharf & Wicket Island,
from The Pine Tree Inn,
Onset, Mass.

The inn constructed a pile wharf for use by its patrons at the foot of Third Avenue (now Admiral's Way). Built at the same time as the inn as an alternate landing to Steamboat Wharf, the 225-foot-long wharf received steamboats virtually at the hotel's front door. It was also used for launches servicing Wicket's and Onset Islands. A March 1, 1914, gale destroyed 80 feet of the wharf.

Pine Tree Inn, Point Independence, Onset, Mass.

Vacationers at the Pine Tree Inn were a mix of the casual and the formal. While bathers enjoyed the beach directly in front of the hotel, more formally attired individuals in shirtwaists and skirts for the ladies and suits for the gentlemen participated in rowing and canoeing. Boating was a popular pastime.

Pine Tree Inn, Onset, Mass.

Besides bathing and boating, Pine Tree Inn guests enjoyed a varied program, as indicated by the *Boston Post* in 1921: "The Pine Tree Inn at Onset has been the scene of many festivities during the summer season, and that famous hostelry is as ever up to its standard." Activities that year included lawn and swimming parties, moonlight excursions, concerts, minstrel shows, a mock marriage, and a mock trial (hopefully unrelated).

Pine Tree Inn, Onset Bay, Mass.

Principal among the inn's attractions, however, was the beach on its doorstep. With 300 feet of frontage directly on Onset Bay, the Pine Tree Inn was the sole hotel at Onset featuring such an amenity. In the 1920s, the hotel was enlarged with a four-story addition, in front of which was constructed a bathhouse for the convenience of the hotel's beachgoers.

Bold Adventurers of the Briny Deep
Point Independence, Mass.

The Pine Tree Inn was promoted as a family hotel. As early as 1913, the hotel advertised itself as "an exceptionally nice place for children, for the beach is within a few feet of the broad piazza and there are clean pine groves between the house and the main road." F.E. Willey was the proprietor at this time, when "Buzzards Bay [had] no more famous summer resort than Onset."

PINE TREE INN, POINT INDEPENDENCE, ONSET BAY, MASS.

The inn also was noted for the dining it afforded both guests and visitors, and part of the hotel's success was attributable to the seafood that it served. In the early 1920s, Chef George H. Ferris required a hogshead of lobsters each weekend to satisfy hungry diners, and he served 60 gallons of clam chowder and an equal amount of fish chowder on Sundays.

Diners were encouraged to eat heartily. According to the *Boston Globe*, "Every guest is asked to eat all he can, to call for as many portions as he pleases of any favorite dishes, to order what he wants if the bill does not suit him, and he can wait to have his special dish prepared. Above all things, a guest is requested not to go away hungry."

The Pine Tree Inn operated seasonally and at its peak had 89 rooms and two rental cottages on Third Avenue. Efforts to modernize included the addition of a cocktail lounge. The hotel survived the postwar era until May 1960, when it was advertised for sale as a going business by the owner who wished to retire. The fire that destroyed it a few years later is well remembered by residents.

Point Independence Club House, Onset Bay, Mass.

Established in 1908, the Point Independence Yacht Club purchased land from the Hammond estate at Seventh Avenue for the location of a clubhouse. Brockton shoe manufacturer Thomas D. Barry, who also served as president of the Brockton Shoe Manufacturers' Association, was named the club's first commodore. Though plans called for both a clubhouse and regular regattas, some unjustly criticized the club's seeming lack of initiative during its first year.

Point Independence Yacht Club from Pier, Onset, Mass.

The club was unfairly mocked by one Boston newspaper in 1908 as "a yacht club without any yachts. It has a lot of land that is paid for, but it has no clubhouse on the land. It has money in its treasury and it is showing a very commendable amount of conservation in the expenditure of that money. It has a commodore who can box shoes better than he can box the compass."

Built at a cost of $4,000, the clubhouse was dedicated on July 3, 1909, and hosted socials and dances, whist parties, and other functions. Yachting naturally remained the principal activity for the club, and both 15- and 21-foot boats were raced. The 21-foot yachts were particular favorites in the waters of Buzzards Bay as they were noted for handling well in all types of weather. (Courtesy of Kenneth R. Maddigan.)

In 1960, the facilities were expanded with a new marina with berths for 28 large boats and 38 heavy moorings. Surviving Hurricane Donna later that fall as well as damage from 23-inch ice during the winter, the club reopened in 1961 with an updated clubhouse. Having proven its 1908 critics wrong, the yacht club remains an important and active organization at Point Independence. (Courtesy of Kenneth R. Maddigan.)

Catholic Church, Point Independence, Onset Bay, Mass.

As early as 1904, the need for a Catholic chapel at Onset was recognized, but not until August 17, 1913, was St. Mary's Star of the Sea dedicated at Point Independence. On October 9, 1924, the original chapel building, the unfinished wooden church being constructed to replace it, and two neighboring cottages were destroyed by arson in the worst fire in Onset's history at that time.

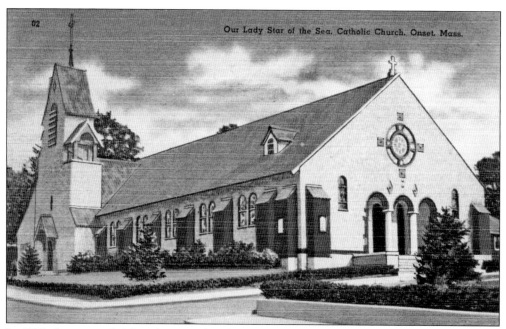

Our Lady Star of the Sea. Catholic Church. Onset. Mass.

In 1925, the present brick and stucco church, St. Mary Star of the Sea Mission, was built with a capacity for 700 worshippers. The church was dedicated with a solemn High Mass on July 12, 1925, presided over by the Most Reverend Daniel F. Feehan, bishop of Fall River. At the time, 1,500 people attended four Masses on Sundays during the height of the summer season.

Fifth Avenue, Onset, Mass.

The view looking south from Hammond Street along Fifth Avenue (now Captain Collis Drive) towards Onset Bay has changed little, though the trees are fewer and the road has been paved. Many of the cottages at Point Independence had Brockton connections, including the extant cottage at Hammond Street and Fifth Avenue (left), which was built in the summer of 1896 by Brockton realtor Lucius Leach. (Courtesy of Kenneth R. Maddigan.)

Sixth Avenue, Point Independence, Mass.

The earliest portion of Point Independence developed was the area south of Hammond Street stretching from First to Seventh Avenues, including 10 lots on Sixth Avenue (now Clearwater Drive). Continuing demand for small cottage lots affordable to the emerging middle class encouraged Job Hammond to later subdivide additional land along the East River. Though most trees in this postcard are gone, the cottages remain and today's view is remarkably similar.

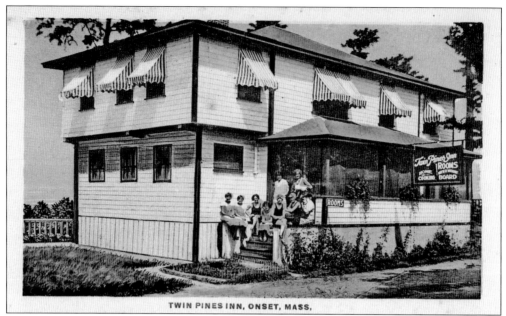

TWIN PINES INN, ONSET, MASS.

Buoyed by the post–World War I boom, Point Independence flourished and smaller inns and boardinghouses were established to accommodate the influx of vacationers. The Twin Pines Inn at the corner of Locust and Holly Streets at Point Independence was one of several examples. Notably, in an era when numerous resort areas and hotels were restricted, many Jews owned cottages at Point Independence, and the Fern Inn welcomed a Jewish clientele.

Maple Street, Point Independence, Mass.

East of Point Independence, other large tracts on Long Neck were developed for summer residences, including Nanumett Heights (245 lots), which contained Maple Street, seen here looking north. Though the area began being developed in the 1890s, the cottages on the right were not built until the 1920s, when they were raised on ground originally reserved as open space by William C. Ramsdell, the developer of Nanumett Heights.

In the easternmost portion of Nanumett Heights, as well as in the adjoining residential subdivisions of Pilgrim Park (82 lots) and Plymouth Park, which were platted in the early 1900s, larger cottages like the ones on Prospect Street (shown here) predominated. To this day, Nanumett Heights remains a closely knit community. (Courtesy of Kenneth R. Maddigan.)

Marking the entrance to Onset Bay, 12-acre Onset Island historically was used by the Swift family for planting, oystering, and pasturage. In 1886, the undeveloped island was acquired by three Brocktonians and surveyed into 124 cottage lots. Due to inconvenience in accessing the island, it developed slowly; by 1911, only seven cottages had been built. Despite severe hurricane damage in 1938 and 1954, the resilient island community persists.

DISCOVER THOUSANDS OF LOCAL HISTORY BOOKS FEATURING MILLIONS OF VINTAGE IMAGES

Arcadia Publishing, the leading local history publisher in the United States, is committed to making history accessible and meaningful through publishing books that celebrate and preserve the heritage of America's people and places.

Find more books like this at
www.arcadiapublishing.com

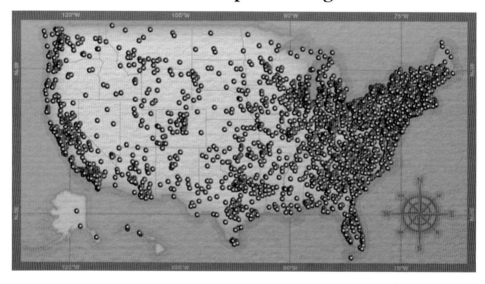

Search for your hometown history, your old stomping grounds, and even your favorite sports team.

Consistent with our mission to preserve history on a local level, this book was printed in South Carolina on American-made paper and manufactured entirely in the United States. Products carrying the accredited Forest Stewardship Council (FSC) label are printed on 100 percent FSC-certified paper.

MADE IN THE USA